# The Holy Spirit
# Whispered In My Ear

## By
## Janie Carter

Unless otherwise indicated, all Scripture referenced is from the King James Version. Scriptures marked KJV are taken from the KING JAMES VERSION (KJV): KING JAMES VERSION, public domain

Scriptures marked NIV are taken from the NEW INTERNATIONAL VERSION (NIV): Scripture taken from THE HOLY BIBLE, NEW INTERNATIONAL VERSION ®. Copyright© 1973, 1978, 1984, 2011 by Biblica, Inc.TM. Used by permission of Zondervan

Cover Design: Noonday Creative, noondaycreative.com

Cover Graphic Elements: Mariia / Adobe Stock, Levskaia Kseniia / Shutterstock, FILINdesign / Shutterstock

# Contents

# Introduction

## The Holy Spirit Whispered in my Ear

"I'm giving you a poem ministry,"
The Holy Spirit whispered in my ear
as I cried out to Him to rescue me
from the bottom of a pit of fear.

My fear was a mother's fear
of losing my first born child.
Sickness had plummeted her
for such a long, long while.

I said, "I don't mean disrespect, Lord;
You know what's in my heart,
but what in the world is a poem ministry,
and how do I give it a start?

He said, "There's a pen and paper in front of you.
Pick it up and I'll show you what to do.
It'll fulfill the most fervent desire of your heart
to be a conduit of my love to impart."

In the next few days I came to understand
as dozens of poems came through my hand;
each designed to minister to a close loved one.
I was taking dictation from the Holy One!

*I'd sometimes be in the shower and I'd start to hear
a special poem message for someone dear.
Then, they started to be messages for the church or
the lost
and the doors opened up to send them across.*

*Now, the time has come to print them in a book.
My prayer is that you will take a look;
that they will bless you and give you joy;
that they will minister to you and your spirit will
soar!*

*Thank You, Jesus!*

# Chapter 1

# Tell Me the Story of Jesus!

## Come Let Us Sing for Joy
## Psalm 95:1, NIV

### Jesus is Lord of Everything (a song)

Jesus is Lord of everything -
Lord of my life, and all that it can bring;
Lord of Summer, Fall, Winter, and Spring.
Jesus is Lord - Lord of everything!

Before I knew Him, I was lost in sin.
Until I knew Him, my life didn't begin.
Praises to His Holy name I'll sing.
Thanks to You, Jesus - I hear eternity ring!

He died on a cross - for you and for me
so that heaven you and I can see -
so that we can always be free.
Thanks to You Jesus - I'm the best I can be!

*He's coming back soon, to carry His children away!*
*I'm looking forward to that sweet day.*
*Until that day comes, I'll serve Him come what may.*
*Because He's Lord - Lord of everything.*
*Oh yes, He's Lord of everything.*
*Yes, He's Lord of everything!*

# Jesus

*Jesus, Jesus*
*Oh, the sound of that wonderful name!*
*It brings such peace to our hearts*
*as we remember why He came.*

*Jesus, Jesus*
*The name the angel to Mary gave -*
*with which to name her little boy*
*because the world He would come to save.*

*Jesus, Jesus*
*All our sins on Him we can lay,*
*and then we'll be seen as pure and clean*
*on that last judgment day!*

*Jesus, Jesus*
*He can live within your heart.*
*Just invite Him in to cleanse you of sin,*
*and His promise is you'll never be apart.*

*Jesus, Jesus*
*You came on Christmas Day -*
*born into a sinful world*
*to take our sins away.*

*Jesus, Jesus*
*You're coming to earth again!*
*Every knee shall bow; every tongue confess*
*that You're Lord over everything!*

*Jesus, Jesus*
*The earth thirsts for Your cup.*
*Come soon in the clouds as You promised*
*and lift, lift us up!*

*Jesus, Jesus*
*The name above all names.*
*Let us be forever with Thee,*
*ever thankful that You came!*

# Christmas is about Love

## NO ROOM IN THE INN

They were tired, cold, and hungry.
Mary was great with child.
Joseph inquired at the inn.
They were turned down without even a smile.

The Son of God - ready to be born
to die in payment for our sins,
and there was no room - no room at all -
no room for Him in the inn.

So, He went where He was welcome -
a lowly stable where the animals lie.
Theirs were the ears that were blessed
to hear the Christ Child's first cry.

Christmas means, "Christ coming."
That first Christmas, few understood -
and for the next two thousand years,
there'd still be few who would.

He was the greatest gift ever given -
God the Father gave His Only Son
to come and dwell among us
with love and forgiveness for everyone.

Will you give Him room this Christmas -
room within your heart?
Will you let Him impart salvation
and give you a brand new start?

Or, if you already know Him -
will you make room for Him with care?
Reach out to the lost and lonely -
the true meaning of Christmas to share?

As we gather with friends and loved ones,
and Christmas bells ring near and afar -
let's praise and worship this Jesus -
the One first found by following a star!

He's coming again real soon, you know -
He's gone now to prepare us a place.
Let's gather in every one whom we can.
In heaven, there's no shortage of space.

Thank You, God, for Christmas -
for sending us Your Precious Son!
Help us to celebrate the way that we should,
with room in our hearts for everyone.

# The Real Meaning of Christmas

Presents, snow, and mistletoe...
good food, good time, good cheer.
It seems like this is all we think about
when Christmas-time is here.

But, what about the Christ Child?
Let's worship _Him_ on Christmas Day.
But, how do we go about that -
what's _true_ worship anyway?

One way is raising our hands -
and singing songs of praise.
But in my heart, there's a thought
of many other ways.

Jesus said, "In as much as ye have done it
unto one of the least of these my brethren,
ye have done it unto Me." *
Let's put something _extra_
underneath that Christmas tree.

Something for the homeless -
for the poor and down-and-out.
Isn't that what Christmas
is _really_ all about?

But you say this recession
has changed the way you live.
This year you don't think
you have anything to give.

How much does it cost to smile
or to lend a helping hand?
Maybe you could listen to someone
and try to understand.

Maybe you could give the gift of forgiveness
to someone against whom you've held a grudge.
Wipe the slate so very clean -
without even a smudge.

How about a simple, "Thank you?"
How about a sincere word of praise?
A hug could lift someone up -
their spirit it would raise.

These are gifts of far more value
than any you could buy.
The Lord will help you with it
if you're only willing to try.

It will add a new dimension
to your Christmas joy and cheer.
And if you keep on giving
you'll have a truly Happy New Year!

*Thank You, God, for letting us*
*be Your hands and feet.*
*If we walk in Your ways*
*You make our life so sweet!*

*\* Matthew 25:40, KJV*

# Mary

An angel appeared to Mary.
His name was Gabriel.
She would conceive and bring forth the Son of God
-
Jesus, the Promised Savior, Emmanuel.

Mary was just a very young girl -
a teenager, as it were.
She pondered these things in her heart.
She was in awe that God had chosen her.

It was too magnificent to understand -
but bless her little heart;
she sent forth praises to the Father
and was willing to do her part.

What about her fiancé, Joseph?
Could he believe this was true?
Just hold on in faith as far as you can;
the Spirit assured her, " I'll take care of you."

He revealed to Joseph that this was true indeed;
an angel spoke to him during a dream.
Joseph followed through with his promise to Mary,
without having to lose esteem.

She journeyed with Joseph to the town of
Bethlehem
to be counted in the census there.
She was about to bring forth her child,
but there was no room, and no one seemed to care.

So, it was in a dirty stable
that Mary delivered her son.
Upon a bed of straw and pain,
the King of King's earthly life was begun.

Mary could hardly contain her joy,
as she held Him to her bosom near.
Looking upon His holy radiant face;
Who He was became crystal clear.

Thirty-three years later,
Mary stood at the cross as He died -
knowing that again, pain was part of the plan
to forgive sin for all mankind.

Then, on Resurrection morning,
she stood in reverence
upon seeing the risen Christ!
It healed even the agony of severance,
it made worth the price.

She had played her part in the Master's plan
of redemption and divine grace.
A mother's part is always crucial
in helping her child to run life's race.

*Blessed are you among women.*
*Thank you, Mary, for pulling through.*
*You could have declined and God would have*
*chosen another -*
*but you let Him <u>use you</u>.*

*Will we, as women, follow Mary's example;*
*do what God beckons us to do,*
*find out what is our calling,*
*and to that calling always be true?*

# It'll Be Christmas Every Day That We're At It

Early on that first Christmas morn;
God the Father sent the world its greatest gift;
it happened in a stable when, the Christ child was
born.
Through His life and death, our sins, He would lift.

It's when we have nothing _but_ this gift of Jesus
that we realize _He_ is enough;
because He's not with us only in good times,
but also when the going gets tough.

It brings the Father much, much, pleasure
to give good gifts to His children each day of the
year;
not just material needs but spiritual ones beyond
measure -
gifts that soften the heart and bring forth a tear.

Christmas is a' coming
and the shoppers are going wild;
we're spending our hard earned money;
we're making the merchants smile.

It's good to carry on the Christmas tradition of
giving,
but materially, we've taken it much too far;
we need to learn from the Lord's example
and bring our spiritual giving up to par.

We need to go into all the world -
sharing this Gospel with everyone.
The Lord commanded us to do this.
It wasn't just a suggestion so a few souls could be
won.

Talk Jesus with everyone you see;
be willing to be called a fanatic.
Let's let the Holy Spirit guide you and me;
It'll be Christmas every day that we're at it.

God gave the gift that keeps on giving -
from here on into eternity.
We need to share His great gift with others,
so they, too, can look to Heaven with certainty.

Salvation's a free gift to us paid for by Jesus the
Son -
so why not just spread it around?
He's coming back soon, it's <u>time</u> that we'd begun
to reach out and cover some ground.

Read the Christmas story to a little child -
Perhaps one who hasn't heard it before -
tell him about God's love with a smile -
It'll be hard to tell which of you will be blessed
more.

*Jesus is the reason for the season;*
*that's a cliché that was popular a few Christmases ago;*
*but we need to make it more than that -*
*get out the message so that all can know.*

*Christmas, oh Christmas- what a wonderful season;*
*It's time to go beyond December 25th*
*with the message of Christ Who's the real reason*
*showing His salvation is not just a Christmas time myth.*

*Guide us, Lord, and give us the power*
*to bring Christmas to others all year with Your love -*
*so that more and more be included in Your family,*
*to spend eternity with You, Lord, up above.*

# What is Christmas?

Christmas is a coming;
and the shoppers are going wild!
But who's taking any time or thought
for Bethlehem's child?

Christmas is God reaching down to touch man
with the tiny hand of His Son.
It's salvation from sin coming to earth -
freedom for all to be won.

It's the promise of resurrection;
in One sent so small;
to grow up, die, and rise from the grave
to answer His Father's call.

Christmas is a mystery.
We can't completely comprehend
how purity and perfection
could totally conquer Satan and sin.

But angels sang
and shepherds gazed in awe;
and wise men knelt before Him
with gifts from afar.

Christmas tries to include so many worldly things -
but Jesus is all it can really be.
He's the answer to all of our problems.
He's the shining light for all to see.

*Thank You, Father, for Jesus*
*and how He came on Christmas Morn.*
*Keep our celebrations in the right perspective -*
*with reverent gratitude for the day He was born!*

# Resurrection
## (We Also Shall Rise Again!)

### Resurrection Morning

Jesus came to seek and save the lost.
He showed only love and kindness along the way.
But, religious leaders had Him nailed upon a cross
on one very dark and dreary day.

If they had only believed who He was,
they wouldn't have mocked Him and taken His
life.
He pleaded, "Father, forgive them for they know
not what they do."*
For He loved them and wanted to spare (even
them) strife.

Thunder rolled and lightening flashed
as He gave up His final breath.
More believed then, who this Jesus had been.
What they hadn't seen in His life, they saw in the
power of His death.

As dreadful as all of this seems,
it was all in God's perfect plan
to bring healing and salvation
from heaven down to mortal man.
Joseph of Arimethea and Nicodemus removed Him
from the cross

and laid Him in a tomb carved out of solid rock.
His mother and many others cried mourning their
loss.
Soldiers rolled a stone blocking the entrance -
serving as a lock.

But no giant stone, hatred or disbelief
could contain the 'Son of God.'
He rose from the grave giving His spirit relief.
He's King of Kings and Lord of Lords!

His mother, Mary, and Mary Magdalene
came to anoint Him on Sunday morn,
but resurrection day had dawned in that grave
yard.
The body of their Lord was gone!

Later, Jesus spoke to Mary Magdalene.
She recognized Him by His voice!
She had thought He was the gardener,
but He was the risen Christ, of course!

What joy! What thrill unspeakable!
The Lord had risen from the grave!
He had defeated sin and death for us.
It was for this His life He gave.

We, too, shall rise from the grave one day
unless we're still living when He returns.
For He ascended into the heavenlies
to prepare a place for us, I've learned.

*Resurrection morning - as it's called,*
*is the focus of all creation;*
*the promise of eternal life in heaven on the other*
*side of the wall.*
*Achieved for us by Jesus' suffering and dedication.*

*Lord, please help us all to see*
*the forgiveness of sin You died to bring*
*and the promise of eternal life to be.*
*Where You, our precious Jesus, will forever reign!*

*\* Luke 23:34, KJV*

# Jesus is Coming Soon!

## *The Signs of the Times*

*The signs of the times*
*are happening everywhere.*
*Apathy is rampant;*
*no one seems to care.*

*It's the "me" generation -*
*Seeking pleasure and seeking fun.*
*We're forgetting God's promise to supply all our*
*needs*
*if we'll just make Him #1.*

*He sent His Son that our joy may be full.*
*He wants to give us the best.*
*But we cast all of that aside*
*and seek after all the rest.*

*Most don't have time for others.*
*The love of many waxes cold.*
*We can forget about loving care*
*if we're ugly, sick, or old.*

*Sometimes, our enemies are of our own household -*
*child against parent or father against son;*
*not even comprehending*
*the loving way a Christian home should be run.*
*People are marrying and giving in marriage*
*just as in the days of Noah.*

Half of those marriages ending in divorce
as worldly pressures rip at the core.

Wars and rumors of wars
are all around the world.
True stories of Christian persecution
are enough to make our hair curl!

There's crime, suffering, disease, and famine
as never seen before.
There are unusual events in the weather -
destroying life and property of the rich and the
poor.

The ridiculous has become acceptable.
Vulgarity and violence entertain.
Young people can yawn while watching on TV
the most vile scenes without any disdain.

Parents clamor for better education and careers
so they can have more material things,
without counting the cost of their family's tears
that quality time away from them brings.

People are searching for peace where there is none,
throwing away treasures while seeking for gold
desperate for love found all too quickly
instead of the kind that's to have and to hold.
Many claim to have the answers
as false religions and cults beckon.
People by the thousands choose to believe a lie
with which one day Jesus will reckon.

None of these happenings should shock us.
Jesus said they'd all come to pass,
and that when we see them we should look up
for our redemption draweth nigh - for our days
are at the last.

Jesus is the answer,
and He's coming soon in the clouds!
Deliverance is close at hand -
the world having had much of what He will allow.

The signs of the end are upon us.
Go tell your family and tell your friends.
Reach out and tell all who will listen.
Tell them repentance mends.

Tell them all about Jesus -
how He died upon the cross;
how He loves them and forgives them
and for their sins paid all the cost.

Tell them all about heaven -
how He's gone a place for us to prepare,
and if they'll receive Him
that they too can be there!
Come Sweet Jesus, come.
Come and take us home with You.
Satan rages and we're miserable here.
Our hearts are torn in two.

*We await with great anticipation*
*the meeting with You in the air!*
*Until then, let the Holy Spirit comfort us*
*and keep us in His care.*

# Hurry! Hurry! Hurry!

Confusion, conflict, and
the devil on the rampage;
as we look around it's easy to see
we're at the very end of the age.

Fear and doubt toss us
this way and that.
Changes happen so fast -
we can't figure what it's all about.

But Jesus has the answer.
He has it all under His control.
The very evil that besets us
keeps God's plan on a roll.

We need to focus on the Great Commission.
There are so many who are still unreached.
We need to follow Billy Graham's example -
making sure the Gospel to all is preached.

Time is short and we're still involved
with all kinds of material things.
Cast that aside, throw it all to the wind,
and see what freedom to witness it brings.

Hurry, Hurry, Hurry!
Reap as many as you can.
With the "Good News" to carry,
help all to understand.

We'll soon be gone without a moment's notice.
Jesus will take us home.
Use the time we have left to rescue others
in whatever places we roam.

Father, we ask for Your wisdom and strength
to carry out Your command.
Supply the tools and weapons we need,
as in Your great army we stand.

Lift us, help us, carry us through.
We'll give all the praise and glory to You.
Holy, perfect, beautiful Savior;
bring each lost soul into Your favor.

We'll all stand there before Your throne,
praising the One who brought us home.
All praise and honor forever more,
to the One above all - we love and adore!

# Chapter 2

# America The Beautiful

## God Bless America

### <u>Do You Have a Heart for America?</u>

Do you have a heart for America?
Will you for her take a stand?
Will you help to spread the Gospel
and turn America around?

Will you help her get back to basics,
to the principles in God's word;
teach by word, deed, and example
a generation who hasn't heard?

America is like an apple -
rotting from the inside out.
Are you willing to root through the rot
to turn the lives of others about?

We are on the verge of losing our freedom.
Immorality always brings a fall.
We're in danger of God's judgment
if we don't answer His urgent call.

God promises to heal the land
of His people who seek His face and pray;
of those who turn from their wicked ways and
repent;
of those who walk the Gospel's way.

Will you help turn back the raging tide;
put your mark on the sands of time;
be a clear sounding bell to a confused generation
with no reason or rhyme?

Are you willing to fight for revival
with the sword of the Spirit and breast plate of
truth?
Are you willing to follow Jesus
like Naomi was followed by Ruth?

Will you have a heart for America?
Will you tell her why Jesus had to die?
Will you tell her about God's grace and love?
Will your heart break for her; will you cry?

God will give you the strength for the battle -
if you'll lay your heart at His feet.
Every weapon will be at your disposal.
Every need He'll be certain to meet.

Lord, give us hearts for America
that hate the sin but love the sinner.
For we know that only through the power of Your
love
can America come forth as a winner!

# "Happy Birthday, America"

Fireworks and hot dogs,
good ole' fashioned apple pie;
we're celebrating America's birthday.
It's the 4th of July!

Founded on God's principles,
She's 242 years old.
We've been blessed to live in America
with blessings untold.

Freedom under her bright blue skies
for all of us who live;
won by countless brave soldiers;
their lives they were willing to give.

There's a church on practically every corner -
a Bible available to every hand;
my eyes mist with tears
when I think of how much I love this land.

Her beauty is breathtaking,
from sea to sparking sea.
Her mountains and her valleys;
God put there for you and me.

Lately, morals have declined
all around the world.
America has been soft and spoiled.
Her values have unfurled.

*But, her greatest asset is her people...*
*I still believe most are strong and true,*
*and that we will join together*
*believing in God to pull us through.*

*Her magnificent flag with the stars and the stripes*
*makes chills run up and down my spine,*
*and I still shed a tear whenever I hear*
*the National Anthem sung each and every time.*

*God Bless America - the red, white, and blue.*
*Continue to guide her every day.*
*Pull her through, ever standing with You,*
*her strength and honor intact, I pray.*

*Amen*

# Chapter 3

# Faith, Hope, Love, and Forgiveness

## Faith

### Warning!
### Don't Neglect So Great a Salvation

If we neglect so great a salvation
when the Bible shows us clear and true;
If we fail to listen to reason;
to surrender our hearts and follow through.

If we fail to pray the sinner's prayer
and humbly be born anew;
If we reject what Jesus did to save us,
then there's no hope for me and you.

No hope we'll live like believers
where God answers our weakest cry;
where He supplies each and every need;
where on Him we can always rely.

There'll be no hope to escape the Great Tribulation
where the antichrist will take rule;
no hope to escape years of torture
when living conditions will be so cruel.
There'll be no hope that we'll go to Heaven;
no hope that we'll escape hell;

no hope that we'll see loved ones again;
or that God will even hear us yell.

Wouldn't it be better to embrace salvation;
to turn the key to the door of new life -
to surrender to the arms of Jesus;
instead of living in selfishness and strife?

Wouldn't it be better to share the Gospel;
to tell others how He shed His blood upon the cross;
to drown our sins in a sea of forgetfulness;
and to remove our guilt - He paid the cost.

Oh what joy it is to follow Him;
to live secure within His embrace;
to have the joy He died to give us;
to help others run _their_ race.

Please don't neglect so great a salvation -
a free ticket into Heaven's gates;
a free stay-out-of-hell ticket
to a life in eternity where the Father waits.

Drop on your knees
and cry out to Him.
Ask Jesus to take away your sin.
He'll answer the smallest call,
and forever be your all and all.
Do it now before it's too late.
Let today be, "your born again date."
"Welcome home My child," you'll hear Him say,
now and also on life's final day.

*Lord, let all who read this poem*
*surrender to the Bible's call;*
*show regret for the sins they commit;*
*and against Satan's wiles stand tall.*

*It's so exciting to have new family in Christ.*
*Help us to guide them along Your path*
*as we take part in Christian fellowship,*
*and learn to love, share, and laugh.*

# The Faith of a Child

Our little girl woke us up
excited because Jesus had spoken to her
to tell her she had been healed
and no more kidney infections would occur!

She had been having them since age two -
after many tests we had found out why.
She had a defective pocket on her kidney.
The chronic pain and nausea would make her cry.

She lived on strong antibiotics.
At age five, she became immune to all.
Her pediatrician had an experimental drug flown
in.
Death for her wasn't God's call.

We tried to tell her she might outgrow it someday.
The doctors had said that was so,
but she was stubbornly declaring what Jesus had
said;
even with symptoms from head to toe.

Her daddy carried in a specimen
the very next morning, you see.
It was negative for the first time in her life.
It was hard to believe it could be.

She had just had her kidney x-rayed,
but we took her for x-rays again.
The doctors couldn't believe their eyes.
The pocket was healed - just a little scar remained!

The antibiotics started making her sick.
We had to stop them, of course.
The Lord had healed our little girl -
to trust Him had been her choice.

It's been many years since then.
We still sing and praise the Lord.
We are so in awe of Him,
the Divine Healer, our loving God!

Thank you, God for healing our child -
for making her life so much better;
for showing her Your healing power
and that you're with her and will never forget her.

# Rest - Under My Wings

You will find Me when you seek Me
with your whole heart.
Putting Me first and praising Me
will be a very good start.

I am the Lord your God.
I love you more than you comprehend.
Keep doing what you believe to be right.
Hold on and My blessings I'll send.

Material goods are temporary.
Time is growing short.
Let your "wish list" be
that there'll be knowledge of ME
in each and every heart.

For you, there will soon be rescue!
Help is on the way!
Until it comes, be calm and still
and trust in Me each day.

Then, your feet will be light.
You'll have a story to share
of My provision and My might;
of My goodness and My care.

*Cast all your cares upon Me.*
*My yoke is easy and I'll carry the load.*
*I'll supply all your needs and then some.*
*Under My wings will be your abode.*

*You are My beloved -*
*one of the most blessed upon this earth.*
*Rest in the love I give you -*
*of immeasurable worth.*

# Our Hope of Heaven!

## They're Watching

In heaven they're waiting for you and me.
The cloud of witnesses above can see
the battles we fight – the race we run;
the ones we lose – the ones that are won.

They cheer us on,
from heaven above.
They watch as we live.
They watch as we love.

They are loved ones who have gone on before.
The pressures of life are not theirs anymore.
Somehow – in some way we don't understand,
they help us down here in this other land.

They're almost through watching
for the day will soon be here –
when we will meet them in heaven
and can hold them near!

Thank you, Lord, for letting them see us –
for letting them share in our lives this way.
May we fight bravely; may we win battles;
may we prove worthy in this final day!

# A Tiny Glow of Hope

We saw a tiny glow of hope,
amidst the black of gloom.
We fought a fearful foe;
we faced the face of doom.

With nary a chance of loss,
for He will see us through;
we battled on and on -
our purpose to ensue.

That tiny glow of hope
has weathered out the storm,
and they rejoice in heaven
to see that all is calm.

## On Streets of Gold

On streets of gold
behind pearly gates;
there for us the Father waits.

In mansions bright
He has for us prepared
a place where He is,
that we may be there.

On streets of gold
in mansions bright;
He'll dry our tears
and make all things right.

Forever with Him
we'll walk those streets of gold
and our loved ones gone before us
we can again closely hold.

We'll serve the Father
and sing praises high -
where there is no sorrow;
where there is no good-bye.

On streets of gold
so I am told;
on streets of gold.

# Daddy's Heavenly Journey

Words can't say
what we feel today;
Our hearts are heavy and sad.

We miss him so.
We have to let him go
and leave only sweet memories
of what together we had.

He's gone from our view,
but his spirit's still true;
just traveling on a new road.

With wonders anew
he's traveling through.
He's a journeyman
in Heaven's abode.

A comfort to our heart
is the glorious thought;
that soon we will see him again.

On that heavenly shore
we'll be together once more;
where there is no suffering or sin.

Thank You, Lord, for Heaven -
for streets of gold and pearly gates;
for Daddy's little mansion on the hilltop
where for all of us he waits.

## Time and Again

### (A message to Christians)

Time and again Jesus comes to you
and whispers in your ear,
Don't let the burdens of life get you down.
Be happy and of good cheer!

Can worry add one day to your life?
Can it change the way things will be?
No - only prayer and faith can do that.
Then you must leave the rest to me.

I take care of the birds of the air
and the lilies of the field.
Isn't it true I've always been there for you
and proven my love to be real?

Time and again I come to you
because you are my child.
You've been a force for good in this world.
You always make me smile!

I see your heart, and it's been taught
to be of service unto Me.
Show compassion and love to others as you ought
and My blessings you'll continue to see.

Put Me first in every little thing.
To every little thing be true,
and I will open the windows of heaven -
pouring out my blessings unto you.

Time and again I come to you
and whisper in your ear,
Watch and be prepared for Me.
My coming is very near.

I want you to stay closed in my arms
like a lamb being carried by a shepherd.
There, you will be safe from all harms
with the One who is most intrepid.

The kingdoms of this world will soon pass away.
Keep your focus on Me.
Just rest easy and let our hearts beat as one,
as you help Me to set sinners free.

Time and again I come to you
and beckon you to come.
Cast all your cares upon Me.
My yoke is an easy one.

Soon I will come and take you home.
It'll be a meeting in the air!
Oh! What a rapture it will truly be -
that where I am, you too will be there!


Look up, for your redemption draweth nigh!
Say to Me, "Come, Lord Jesus, Come."
I'll be appearing in the sky -
the King of Kings - The Everlasting, Holy One!"

## Me and My Daddy

Before I could know him, Lord
You took him away.
We didn't have time for laughter,
We didn't have time for play.

He was the only Daddy, Lord,
that I could ever have.
You know how I feel deep inside;
You know how hurt – how sad.

Please keep him in Your loving care,
till I come there with him,
and we will talk, and we will share,
and we can love again.

And, as I walk down here on earth
until that sweet day comes...
keep my pathway straight, Dear Lord,
and thanks for all You've done.

# Love

## <u>Treasures of the Heart</u>

What are the treasures of a Christian's heart?
Let's look inside and explore.
Of all the good things that God imparts,
love seems to be at the core.

Love is Jesus, and Jesus is love.
He's the treasure who sits on the throne
within the heart of a Christian and pours forth
love
wherever that person may roam.

Love always goes the extra mile -
even when dealing with an enemy -
will return a scowling gaze with a smile -
when there's work to do, says, "Send me!"

First Corinthians 13 says a lot about love.
It says it's patient, kind, and true.
It's always ready to forgive.
It has time for me and you.

It's understanding and not demanding.
It's unselfish, humble, and pure.
It's quick to say, "I'm sorry."
to bring to misunderstanding a cure.

*It always sees the good in others -*
*the silver lining in the darkest cloud.*
*It praises the blessings of Jesus!*
*It never gives up and doesn't need to be proud.*

*Love gives to others even when in personal need.*
*Then happiness fills the heart!*
*When fairly corrected, will take heed,*
*and try to do what it ought.*

*A mature heart will reach out in kindness -*
*putting another's feelings first -*
*will sacrifice when need be -*
*with affection will almost burst!*

*A Christian's heart throbs in pain*
*to see others outside the Kingdom of God -*
*will work at every opportunity to gain*
*souls for Jesus, no matter how hard.*

*You might ask, "How can I have a heart*
*like the one you've just described?"*
*Just make Jesus the King of your heart.*
*A child of the King is never of love deprived.*

*He'll fill your heart with such good things -*
*the bad things will have no room.*
*Blossoms of love and goodness -*
*will be everywhere in bloom!*

*Thank You, Lord, for giving us hearts*
*that can be used to dispense Your love.*
*Keep filling us with the Holy Spirit -*
*sent from up above.*

# Love the Children

Little girls are made of sugar and spice and
everything nice
or so the saying goes.
Boys are made of frogs and snails and puppy-dog
tails
and all other kinds of woes.

But we know that they're truly made
in the image of God himself.
Children are a beautiful gift to us
greater than any material wealth.

Jesus said, "Suffer the little children to come unto
me
and forbid them not:
for of such is the kingdom of God." *
Oh my! He sure loved them a lot!

The Bible says, "He was much displeased,"
when His disciples turned them away.
He is still very, "much displeased"
when anything separates them today.

A child needs the arms of Jesus.
Don't let anything come in between.
Too much TV or too many worldly things
can be the kinds of things I mean.

A child needs to walk and talk with Him
and to listen for His reply.
He needs to praise and to read His word
to find the reasons why.

Most are so full of joy and fun;
their laughter fills the air.
Like sunshine flooding a darkened room;
their joy is everywhere.

Their little hearts are tender -
ready to receive, to care, to love.
Their little minds are eager
to learn more of the Father above.

Then, there are the sad ones -
abused, neglected, or in despair.
They need to be able to see in us
a loving God who will care.

So, reach out and love the children.
You'll reap a hundred-fold.
They are the hope of our future.
They'll be the leaders when we are old.

Father, we know that inside our hearts;
in each and every one;
there lives a little child -
Your daughter or Your son.

*Yes, we are all Your children;*
*all of us who've been born again.*
*Thank You for receiving us as a little child*
*to be saved from our sin.*

*\* Mark 10:14, KJV*

# The Ladies' Retreat

Over the hills and through the woods
to the country farm we went.
Now that it is in the past,
we can't believe all our time has been spent.

The owners were lovely hosts,
and the meals they served were delish.
For a better place to have retreat
you just couldn't wish.

We were filled with anticipation
for what the Lord would do.
We looked to Him with open hearts
and let His love pour through.

We laughed, we cried, we sang, we shared,
we ministered to each other.
We read His Holy Word, we cared,
we prayed for our sister and brother.

We learned that the blood of Jesus
covers all of our sin;
that we can use it's power
and over Satan we can win.

We learned to put tradition aside
and to obey the voice of God;
and that if we let God's Spirit fill us,
handling problems won't be so hard.

*It was sort of like a bridal shower,*
*for we are the bride of Christ.*
*He showered us with His love and power,*
*for He's already paid the price.*

*Many old hurts and grievances*
*were wiped clean off the slate.*
*God's healing balm touched us all*
*and many healings took place.*

*And then, on the funnier, lighter side;*
*two hilarious ladies were there.*
*At bedtime, they kept us in stitches -*
*there was sleeplessness everywhere!*

*We thank You, Lord, for our families*
*who took care of things at home*
*so that we could go, relax, and enjoy -*
*knowing that all was done.*

*And we thank You, Lord, for a retreat*
*where we were in one accord;*
*but most of all for our Savior so sweet -*
*our most precious living Lord.*

## Go Light the World

There's a lost and dying world out there.
They need the love of God.
We need to take it to them,
and with the Holy Spirit's help, it won't be so hard.

We have the light of Jesus
within our hearts and in our minds.
If we ask, He'll give us direction
to carry it to all mankind.

We have to care and love enough
to resist Satan's war against the light.
We have to be brave and willing
to carry on and not give up the good fight.

We need to love to tell the story
of Jesus and His love.
We need to share what He's done for us -
how He brought salvation from the Father above.

And then we need to bare our hearts
and tell them our personal story -
how if they repent, He'll forgive any sin.
So, there's no need for them to worry.

Even the tiniest light
will expel the darkest night,
and if we'll put our lights together,
we can shine with a love so bright!

We need to march onward as Christian soldiers
for time is running so short, you know...
using the light of Jesus
to make the Kingdom of God grow.

Lord, help us to light our world
each and every day.
Give us the desire, the strength and the love
to shine for You all along the way.

# Forgiveness

## Love Never Dies

Love may go on life support,
but love never dies, my friend.
From the moment it ignites within your heart,
it never ever, ever ends.

It may become bruised and offended.
It may become as cold as stone.
It may resemble hate more than affection -
the thin line between the two being prone.

But with just a touch of The Holy Spirit,
it can spring forth again and flood the heart.
Oh, what an apology can produce
when coming from the heart's most tender part.

Pride often keeps reconciliation from happening.
Nobody ever seems to want to admit he's wrong,
but pride is a cold, cold, companion,
and loneliness just feels wrong.

And when pride goes with you to heaven's gate
God's heart will break when He turns you away;
if you haven't forgiven all others
as in the Lord's prayer Jesus taught us to say.

He taught that we'll be forgiven our debts
exactly as we forgive our debtors.
Even those who aren't sorry included in that
group;
which certainly wouldn't be <u>our</u> druthers.

So actually, forgiveness is not an option
if you want the Father to forgive you.
He makes it clear within His Word.
He clearly says it's true.

So let The Holy Spirit give you the strength
to apologize or to accept one from another.
It'll be amazing the surge of love you will feel
as you look into the eyes of your sister or brother.

Your heart will dance as God restores the love
that forgiveness brings about.
You'll want to sing praises to the Lord above.
You'll feel like you want to shout!

Father, we want to thank You
for only You can mend our hearts,
and restore relationships to their original glory
which in turn blesses You as we ought.

# Peace Can Reign Within Your Heart

Jesus said that it would be impossible
for offenses not to come;
but with the Holy Spirit within us;
we don't have to anger succumb.

Out of your pain, peace can reign
if you let obedience and love rule.
Jesus said to be angry but sin not -
the Bible being the textbook for the Holy Spirit's
school.

"But" you say, "it's just not fair.
You don't know what they did to me,
and after all I've done for them.
I guess you just can't see."

Pride sets in, and we put up a wall.
The Bible calls it a stronghold.
"They won't hurt me again," you say.
"I'll never forgive. Let everyone be told."

But we're supposed to follow Jesus' example
and let love and forgiveness in our heart reside
keep anger and hate at bay.
For all it does is truly divide.

*They say that to err is human,*
*but to forgive is divine.*
*Jesus tells us in the Lord's Prayer*
*we'll be forgiven as we forgive others - in kind.*

*Jesus also tells a parable about a man*
*who was forgiven much and didn't have to pay,*
*but refused to forgive another*
*and had his forgiveness taken away.*

*That's what God wants to show us -*
*that forgiveness is not an option*
*if we want to receive forgiveness*
*and into God's family - adoption.*

*When we choose complete humility -*
*to let go and love like we've never been hurt;*
*peace floods our hearts and gives us tranquility*
*to give our relationships a brand new start.*

*Thank You, Jesus for being our example*
*of how to love and how to forgive.*
*Help us to stay humble and forgiving*
*for as long as on this earth we live.*

# With the Same Measure You Judge, You Will Be Judged

Oh, the pain and ridicule we suffer
when we try to do our best.
It's as if life is trying
to put us to some distorted test.

The Bible tells us not to judge,
for we can't know another's heart.
Just to love and try to understand -
that's to be our part.

So, we take it to the feet of Jesus,
and in a crumpled heap we leave it there.
There our wounds will be healed.
There we've found He who will care.

Jesus, You know how it feels
to be misunderstood.
Help me to respond to my accusers
in the way that I should.

How many times have I misjudged others
and caused them grief and pain?
The thought that I must have done this
brings my heart to shame.

Lord, help me to remember
the shock and bewilderment that I feel.
The pain of being falsely accused
is very, very, real.

And help me to remember
to give the benefit of the doubt -
to go directly to the person
and find the truth of what it's all about.

In other words, help me to be more like You -
to understand and to forgive;
to be an oasis of Your love
for as long as on this earth I live.

# Chapter 4

# By The Holy Spirit's Power!

## Praise Him!

### As In His Light We Take Our Stand

"The people that walked in darkness
have seen a great light." *
Isaiah prophesied of Jesus -
born that first Christmas night.

His light revealed the hearts of men.
It guides our path - it exposes our sin.
It shows us all what we might have been
without the grace of God.

It shows us, clearly, salvation's door
and the way to eternal life.
How could we ever ask for more -
eternal freedom from death and strife?

There's now a darkness coming on the earth
like there's never been before.
Satan's gathering his forces -
he wants the winning score.

But Bethlehem's Babe -
Who died on a cross and rose out of the grave
will split the eastern sky.
The light will be bright, and He will be beheld
by each and every eye.

It's good to walk in His light -
in the refuge of His power and might;
holding on tighter than tight -
as this new year emerges.

The darkness will not envelop us -
in Him we have faith - in Him we have trust.
We'll be safe in the hollow of His hand -
as in His light we take our stand
and as this dark world He purges.

So, through the darkened days ahead -
by His light will we be led -
'til He comes to judge the quick and the dead -
we'll be shining lights for Jesus.

The harvest is ripening;
the workers are few -
the evening shadows are all askew.
Let's shine our lights for Jesus.

Lord, 'til You come to earth again -
we'll be walking in Your light.
Keep the darkness away from us -
help us to fight the good fight.
Help us to labor in the harvest field -

to come rejoicing, bringing in the sheaves -
to overcome the darkness -
which only Your light relieves.

* Isaiah 9:2, KJV

## Holy Spirit Thou Art Welcome!

Holy Spirit, Thou art welcome in this place.
We need Your Presence;
and Your power;
to help us run the race.

We want to roll up our sleeves, Lord,
and go to work for You.
Please give us the vision
for what You'd have us do.

Let us minister to each other.
Come and cleanse our inner pain.
Remove old hurts and grievances
that would tend to remain.

Create in us a clean heart -
joy in our salvation anew.
Give us a strong foundational bond
as we attempt our job for You.

Let us remember the importance of prayer -
conversation, Lord, with You.
Guide us with that still small voice.
Keep us kind and true.

We want to put tradition aside
and follow the leading of Your voice.
We want to study Your Holy Word
in running out our course.

We want to stomp all over Satan
in the power of Jesus' name.
Tough love with perseverance
will put all evil to shame.

We want to call on the blood of Jesus
not only to cover our sins,
but to loose others who are in bondage.
Only with its power can we win!

We know we're fighting a mighty battle.
Sounds onerous for a church ladies' group.
But we know time is short and in our hearts
we know we can be quite a troop!

Let us have fun in the doing -
finger sandwiches and laughs to enjoy;
sharing the work and fellowship -
lighthearted joy to employ!

You're love. You're the Spirit of Jesus;
we want to be His hands.
Fill us, please, Holy Spirit -
our hearts' desires You understand.

Let the fragrance of our love fill the church
and be carried to others beyond.
Keep us enfolded in Your wings -
ever free from harm.

*Put us in one accord*
*as we praise and lift You high.*
*Oh Beautiful Dove, give us love;*
*higher than the sky!*

# Do We Need a Prayer Language?

Do we need a personal prayer language?
Well, just let us see -
Would you need a butter knife
or a chain saw to cut down a big oak tree?

Maybe a bulldozer would be needed
to clear a forest of those trees.
Maybe a prayer language which
bypasses Satan's knowledge is needed
while you're doing spiritual warfare upon your
knees.

Certainly it's a tool that's needed
to get God's work done here on earth.
Certainly you can be God's hands
while you still walk this turf.

Surrender your voice in prayer to Him.
He will do the rest.
Tell Him that you want this tool.
That He'll give it to you, I can attest.

He wants the great commission fulfilled -
a prayer language can help to get that done.
There's power of the Holy Spirit in it -
sent for use to us by Jesus the Son.

There's deep, sweet communion in it -
certainly nothing to fear.
Sometimes we know not what we pray
then the Holy Spirit prays for us to God the Father
and makes it clear.

It's not something spooky or kooky.
It's simply a tool to be used.
Satan would have us reject it.
He would want us to be confused.

But Jesus always trumps Satan.
He wants the Holy Spirit to comfort us and give us
joy.
A prayer language gives us peace
and prayer power to employ.

Jesus, let us use all the gifts You offer us
as we aspire to do Your work along life's way.
Then any crowns we receive at Your judgment
seat
we can choose to cast at Your feet one day!

# Chapter 5

# Hard Times and Healing

## Trust Him

### The Agony of Estrangement

My heart's in despair;
I can't sleep.
Just below the surface,
I weep and weep.

The tears spill over -
I want to die.
Only God knows my pain.
Only God hears my cry.

It's the middle of the night;
it's the middle of the day.
It makes no difference -
it never goes away.

My mind searches for answers
as I relive the past;
all the joys of yesterday
that didn't last.

What happened between us?
When went wrong?
Why does my soul
sing such a sad song?

Doesn't love cover
a multitude of sins?
Doesn't forgiveness
let new life begin?

Lord, come and heal
my pain and my grief;
as I cry out
for some kind of relief.

Help me to go on –
 to feel joy anew.
I'll give all the praise
and glory to You.

We can't do it alone
in our human state.
For Your healing balm...
I'll wait -

Jesus, come.

## The Day I Died!
## (My Testimony)

*I want to die!*
*I just want to die.*
*That was my every thought.*
*The pain was so intense, I couldn't cry.*
*Only craving for death filled my heart.*

*I felt I couldn't change my mind.*
*I just wanted to die so much.*
*How could I know that I was about*
*to feel the Master's touch?*

*As I held my hands to the sides of my head,*
*a cry from my soul tore loose.*
*"Oh God, help me," is what I said*
*as tears flooded my face profuse.*

*I stumbled to my feet and tripped*
*on a little book lying there.*
*How could it be out of place?*
*I had straightened the room with such care.*

*I had given a blind man a quarter*
*for that book as a little girl.*
*How could I know that that little book*
*held the most precious words in the world?*

It was a little book of Bible verses,
and I opened it and read;
"For whosoever shall call upon the name of the
Lord
shall be saved," it said.

"Could that mean me?" I asked God,
for on His name I had just called.
I'd always wanted to know how to be saved,
but I couldn't believe that could be all.

And then, something supernatural happened.
The period enlarged and came up off the page.
It was God's way of showing me
that was all I had to do to be saved.

A feeling of calming peace surrounded me.
I'd never seen anything supernatural before.
I started jumping up and down thanking the Lord
that I was saved and going to heaven for sure.

Satan had been defeated.
God had won the victory!
Then, for the first time in my life,
I heard God speaking clearly to me.

He gave me a list of family names
that He said through me would be saved.
I've referred to that list time and again
as the way for each one He has paved.
He also gave me a feeling
of water flooding my body inside,

as I asked Him to forgive me
for all my sins, and I cried and cried.

Surely, I did die on that day.
I died to self and sin.
But to a new life I was born.
I was truly born again!

I could feel the Holy Spirit rejoicing with me.
This was an answer to my prayers.
It felt so wonderful; I was free.
I needed nothing else; Jesus was there!

Jesus - oh Jesus! What a friend He's been!
My Savior, my Lord - all His promises He's kept.
You see, it's been fifty years since then,
and He's walked with me daily - step by step.

Dear Lord, I can't thank You enough
for saving me on that day.
Thank You for dying in my place
and for showing me the way.

I love You, Lord Jesus!

# Whole Once Again

What's almost as painful as death
is a family that's left
to face the onslaught of
the world's problems alone.

No husband or father to protect
or even to direct.
His wife and children's lives he neglects
and doesn't even hear their moans.

Oh, let God's Spirit get through
and make his heart anew.
Open his ears to their pain.

They're ready to forgive and forget.
They still love him yet.
They can still be a family again.

The blood of Jesus forgives
and for as long as he lives,
he can draw strength for the fight
from this blood.

His marriage is broken and lost
but at the foot of the cross
love can come pouring back in like a flood.

They can work hand in hand.
He can take a stand like a man.
He can be strong and whole once more.

*Lord, cradle this family in Your care.*
*Let them know that You're there -*
*always mending their hearts from the core.*

*Joy and happiness returned;*
*many lessons will have been learned.*
*Praise Your name for forgiveness of sin.*

*We'll know it was You*
*because it is surely true;*
*only You can make whole once again!*

# God Heals in Many Ways

I have a disease call Sarcoidosis or Sarc for short,
but the good news is, it'll never have me.
If the Lord doesn't heal me one day,
I'll continue to fight to be the best I can be.

I've had it all of my life,
but wasn't diagnosed until age sixty-one.
I'm glad I didn't know it had a name.
I may have to fearfulness succumbed.

Medicine helped a whole, whole lot.
I only had to take it for less than two years.
It reversed my symptoms somewhat -
giving me many more years!

Carrying infections so much as a preemie
and ruptured appendix at only age three,
the doctors kept me full of antibiotics
and destroyed my immune system, you see.

I think God used it to make me a fighter -
to push through no matter how hard.
It was usual for me to be sick a lot,
but I was determined to live a normal life, thank
God.

*A wonderful marriage, three beautiful daughters,*
*three great, "sons" who married them - what joy!*
*Then, three darling grandchildren*
*(including the sweet one who married my*
*grandson)*
*and two precious great grands - oh boy!*

*I was able to teach Sunday school and Missionettes*
*and take care of some of the elderly in the family.*
*God helped me to pull through - able to do*
*all I dreamed of without any personal health*
*calamity.*

*God healed a partially detached retina for me*
*about two years ago while watching prayer on 700*
*Club - CBN.*
*I expect He might do the same with the Sarc.*
*only this time through a pre and probiotic regime.*

*The good bacteria in the probiotic, yogurt, and*
*some foods*
*puts your immune system back into balance.*
*God uses many ways His miracles to perform.*
*Sometimes natural things will meet the challenge.*

*I believe the supernatural should be natural to*
*believers.*
*I've experienced it so many times throughout my*
*life.*
*He puts our belief to the test - our fears He arrests*
*as we trust Him to calm our woes and strife.*

*Thank you, Father, for always loving me -
for being with me through all of life's trials.
Help me to be strong - to choose right over wrong
and to believe Your word about healing with no
denials.*

*Praise You, God!*

# Life - Don't Give Up On It

There's a famous poem written that tells us not to quit,
but I'm writing another one to wit.
Enough can't be said about not giving up.
At the end of the road, there's a Victor's cup.

I have a question I'd like to pose:
why does life crush the sweetest rose?
Is it true that only the strong survive?
Or do we all have a chance as long as we're alive?

Whether strong or weak, we must go on.
There's a time to die, just as there's a time to be born.
We must rest easy in our Maker's arms,
and not succumb to the world's alarms.

We must thank Him each morning when we arise
and learn to enjoy the good and the bad, not to despise.
For the Bible tells us both are used by the hand of God.
When we realize this, problems aren't as hard.

We must carry on when depressed and grieved,
and keep expecting relief until we've received;
lay our heads on the pillow each night and rest,
knowing we're passing life's greatest test.

*After every night, the morning must come.*
*There'll be joy in the morning, with the morning*
*sun.*
*So, rise up and surge ahead each day.*
*Never give up because it doesn't pay.*

*My prayer for you is that you go on*
*to win the Victor's cup and sing a song:*
*a song of praise, a song of love,*
*with others here and the Lord above.*

*Don't let troubles get you down -*
*even when you feel like you're gonna drown.*
*Jesus is there to pull you up.*
*The Victor's cup is an overflowing cup!*

*Lord, turn our frowns into smiles.*
*Help us to go on these last few miles*
*until You come to earth again,*
*and we'll say, "Worth it all, it has been!"*

*Amen*

# Chapter 6

# The Light Side

## God has a Sense of Humor!

### Little Things

It's the little things that bother me...
sometimes so small, I cannot see.
You might ask, "How can that be?"
Well, just let me tell you...

Little disobediences and little sins,
send me down the path that cannot win.
Teach me, Lord, to obey You
and in every little thing be true.

It's when little tempers flare,
and nothing seems to be quite fair;
I wonder when - I wonder where,
we'll ever learn to love and share.

It's the little stinging bees -
Oh, why don't they stay up in the trees?
Or my child falls down and skins her knees;
it's the little things that bug me!

*Lord, don't let the little things build up,*
*and keep your blessings from filling my cup.*
*Keep my heart pure and white -*
*so that I'm pleasing in Your sight.*

*Amen*

# Charlie and Joe

There's a joke about two friends -
their names are Charlie and Joe.
Charlie is always having bad luck,
and he always wants Joe to know.

"It could be worse," Joe always says,
"Just pull yourself up and go on ahead.
I'd just ignore it if I were you.
Nobody wants to be around somebody who's blue."

Then one day, Charlie's house burned to the
ground,
and Joe said the usual thing.
Charlie said, " Now wait just one minute, my
friend.
What in the world worse could bad luck bring?"

As always, Joe was quick to answer.
"It could be my house, he said with a grin."
At this point, the joke's punch line
comes to an abrupt end.

You're left to ponder that last line -
if trouble comes to others, we think all is fine.
We only understand when it happens to us,
and then we want others to make a big fuss.

*The Golden Rule from the Bible should come into play.*
*We should do unto others each and every day*
*what we would want done unto us with love,*
*and oh how that would please the Father above!*

*Speaking of You Father, I want to say,*
*"Thank You for being here for us each day."*
*Because sometimes, being human, we let each other down,*
*but You always give us hope and take away our frowns.*

# V.B.S.

Our Vacation Bible School was so much fun.
It seemed to be over almost before it was begun.
We learned about Jesus and how He rescues us.
Our 911 calls to Him in prayer is a must.

Jesus to the rescue - Life Call 911.
If we believe and repent, He saves us from the
chains of sin
and forgives all the wrong we've done.

He heals us when we're sick
and calms the wind and sea.
He even rescues us from death
and gives Heaven to you and me.

We had so much fun in the learning.
We sang new songs and worked puzzles through.
We went to the rescue squad room
where we made a neat craft each day, too.

There were many winners in the coloring contest
and yummy snacks each day.
On Friday, we had a picnic
and, until it was over, the rain stayed away -
hooray!

*Everyone seemed to enjoy it -*
*the children, teachers, and helpers alike.*
*Jesus smiled upon us*
*and made everything turn out right.*

*Thank you, Lord, for granting us*
*a wonderful week at V.B.S.*
*Help us to remember to call upon you, 911*
*when life puts us to the test.*

# Chapter 7

## Family

### Parents

### <u>Family</u>

Having a close family
brings both joy and pain,
but I can surely tell you
it's worth it all the same.

Just having family to share and care
whatever comes your way,
and knowing that they are there
in case of a rainy day.

Sometimes we irritate each other
or criticize our sister or brother,
but just think of how it would be
if you had no family.

Someone has said that loneliness
wouldn't be so bad
if you had someone to share it with -
it wouldn't be so sad.

*But loneliness is a sad thing,*
*to stand alone is hard.*
*I've never had to feel that pain,*
*and I'd like to thank the Lord.*

*So, just remember when sister Sue*
*or Aunt Mary gets your goat -*
*that love covers a multitude of sins,*
*and family love is what it's all about!*

# Daddy's Little Girl

"You're the end of the rainbow,
you're my pot of gold."
That's how he felt about me,
as the words he sang told.

We also sang together -
"South of the Border" was the one.
We weren't great or famous,
but boy - we sure had fun!

I'd run to meet him in the evenings
as he'd bring the truck to park.
His arms were tight around me,
and we'd talk and talk and talk.

He'd sit and teach me right from wrong,
and I'd listen all the way.
Some of the lessons he taught me
are values I have today.

He worked hard and brought me up,
and I'm a woman now,
I've given him grandchildren
and also some gray hair.

My heart is filled with gratitude,
my eyes are filled with tears,
as I recall all the love
he's shown me through the years.

*Lord, he's growing older now,*
*and I ask, "How do I begin*
*to show him I'm still his little girl*
*just like I've always been?"*

*Thank you for my daddy, Lord,*
*and all he's meant to me.*
*Keep him in Your loving care*
*until Your face he'll see.*

## My Mama

She loved me right from the start
way down deep within her heart -
in the most tender part.
That's how my mother loves me!

She'd give her very life for me,
but she did more than that, you see.
She lived for me day by day,
and no matter what - loved me anyway.

All mistakes we made will pass away,
but the love we share is here to stay.
She'll love me onward - come what may.
That's how my mother loves me!

We've had good times together -
shopping in the stores,
and no matter how much she gives;
she wants to give me more.

Lord, I saw her on her knees in prayer,
as she lifted up to You her cares;
when I was small and she was young.
That's when my talks with You were begun.

She is growing older now,
and a little gray streaks her hair.
I ask that over her You'll take care,
and your Holy Spirit will hover;
that's how much I love my mother!

# Marriage

## <u>My Loving Husband</u>

You lift me up when I am down.
You dry each tear; you erase each frown.
You chase away my fears with words so wise,
and teach me that each problem can be a blessing
in disguise.

How could I make it through a day without you,
without your smile, a wink, and your love so true,
without the quick telephone call just to tell me the
love you feel
or invite me out to lunch to enjoy a good meal?

The answer is that it would be hard to make it
through,
my life depends so much on you.
I know you're there for me come rain or shine.
Thank the Lord, I know that you are mine!

You're just too good for your own good,
always working hard to help others.
You would always be on the giving end
if you could have your druthers.

"The Good Lord and then the family come first,"
that's what you always say.
You work so hard to take care of us
each and every day.

You want to share everything you have,
inviting the family over to eat,
and when you've worked your culinary magic
the food is always quite a treat!

I know you, and I know
that right now you'd be a wishin'
that you could get away for a little while
and go to the river to do some fishin'!

You're a very special person,
and I'm so glad God gave me you
to travel with down the road of life,
so I'd be happy instead of blue.

A good husband is hard to find.
They're few and far between,
but I had help from Jesus.
His cupid skills are keen!

Thank You Lord, for my husband.
Bless him every day.
Protect him, guide him, give him joy,
all along life's way.

# A Lifetime of Love

There is a wedding day coming
that will change two into one.
My daughter will be the bride that day,
and her groom will become my son.

Their love has been tested,
and proven strong and true.
Together with the Lord above,
they're ready to face the new.

Time stands still when a bride appears;
all stand and look her way.
For this is the day she seals her love…
on this her wedding day.

The groom is such a special guy.
They were truly made for each other.
His love for my daughter is precious;
an answer to prayer for this mother.

They seal their love with vows and a kiss.
Each gives the other their heart;
as they promise to love come what may…
until death do they part.

Yes, Lord, their lives will truly change
from this shining day on.
May you give them a lifetime of love,
and may that love continue strong.

## Honeysuckle Still Blooms Sweet

Fifty-five years ago, my parents married,
then, went on a honeymoon.
They came home to a room full of honeysuckle
the bride's dad had found in bloom!

They've had many ups and downs
throughout their married life.
But through it all, they were in for the long haul,
and they made it as husband and wife.

They've known what in life is most important:
God, then family takes first place;
children and grandchildren abundant -
their house hardly has enough space.

The Bible is our yardstick of what spells success
and my parents accomplished this feat.
Their children rise up and call them blessed,
and the honeysuckle still blooms sweet.

## "Let's Take a Mini-Moon"

"I'd love to take a mini-moon,
and honey, could we take it soon?
I'd love to be alone with you
to do the silly things we do.

We could go bargain hunting
at yard sales and flea marts;
and look at the beautiful Fall leaves;
which always touch our hearts.

Let's stop and get a hot dog
at a little country store;
take our time, as the hills we climb.
Who could ask for more?

Maybe the most special part
is the conversation we share.
I can always look into your eyes
and tell that for me you care.

Let's not forget the apples
we always buy and bring back home.
They're a little taste of where we've been
when together we roam.

Being alone together
is a special part of our life.
It helps us to remember it can be fun
just being husband and wife!

# Joys of Parenting!

## A Mother's Love

A mother's love -
what can compare?
Certainly nothing
on this earth anywhere.

It's deeper than the ocean.
It's higher than the skies.
It's a sacrifice of self -
to self, a mother truly dies.

From the time she feels that first tiny flutter,
within her womb so deep -
until she takes her own last breath -
love for her child in her heart she does keep.

It compares only with the love of Jesus
because it's unconditional and true.
It looks at the child and sees the good -
yet understands the shortcomings, too.

If a mother has more than one child -
she loves each one the same.
And if her children don't realize this,
it's just sibling rivalry that's to blame.

A mother's love cuddles in warm blankets
and sings a lullaby.
It gets up at 2 a.m.
It hears the slightest cry.

It delights when Baby's first word is "DaDa",
although "MaMa" is _her_ name.
It's there to guide the first small step -
it's there to play a game.

A mother's love teaches of Jesus -
with her child at her knee.
It wants the child to grow strong and tall,
and a Christ-like spirit it wants to see.

The first day of school is a hard one,
but love learns to let go.
She sends her child off with a prayer in her heart
that this child will grow up slow.

But growing slowly is not the way of children.
So, a mother's love learns to keep the pace.
Peanut butter sandwiches, sports, youth meetings
at church,
and homework all enter the race!

Then all so suddenly the running is over.
The child has learned to drive a car!
Then that magic age, "18"-
"adult" according to law.
College, marriage, and their own children -
the changes all happen so fast.

But the mother's love doesn't change.
It was created by God to last!

Then the mother is also a grandmother -
and oh, the love that is there!
She reaches out so tenderly -
a blend of her wisdom and love to share.

Thank You, Lord, for a mother's love -
for patterning it after Your own,
and that children can carry it in their hearts -
even long after they've grown!

Amen

## About Dads

Any man can become a father,
but it takes someone special to be a "Dad."
I'm glad to say that the latter one mentioned
is the kind I've always had.

A "Dad" hardly notices how hard he works
for the benefit of his child.
He comes home bone-tired,
but will play for, "just a little while."

He's directly responsible to Jesus
for the condition of his entire household.
He prayerfully leads and disciplines -
and sees that his child does what he is told.

He's strong and yet he's gentle -
understanding and fair.
In the good times and the bad -
for his child, he's always there.

His children feel secure in his love.
They know he'll try to do what is right.
They know he's leaning on Jesus -
every day and night.

His daughter is his "Little Princess."
His son is his "Little Man."
He tries to be the very best
role model that he can.

The advice he gives his child is priceless -
born of experience and care.
He wants the very best for his child.
His time and wisdom he's willing to share.

It's difficult for him to see his children
make their own mistakes,
but when they do, he helps them back on track...
doing whatever it takes.

He sets aside his own ego.
He sets aside his pride -
and gives acceptance and forgiveness -
flowing deep and wide.

It's hard for him to give his daughter away
to marry another man,
but the fact that she's still "his little girl,"
is just something she must understand.

He passes onto his son all he knows -
by example and by word,
and he's very, very, proud of him...
in case you haven't heard.

As a grandad, his patience and love are
remarkable
or that's how it surely does seem.
He takes his grandchildren for piggy-back rides
and out for their favorite ice cream.

*Thank You, Lord, for our dads -*
*Bless them every one.*
*Let them feel the satisfaction...*
*of such an important job well done!*

*Amen*

# Me Monster

You might ask, "What is a Me Monster?"
Well, you were born with one inside of you!
The lil' monster will do anything to get its way.
It's determined to do whatever it wants to do.

Hopefully, our parents try to tame it.
Oh yes, I have a Me Monster, too.
We all do because we're human.
It's the state of humanity - it's true.

We kick, we cry, we're tempted to tell a lie.
We want what we want _now_!
We think if we don't get it, we'll die.
We're about to have a _cow_!

The Bible says to spare the rod
is to spoil the child.
Parents need to discipline us
so we won't just grow wild.

Nothing is more beautiful
than a child who's loving and sweet,
but still permitted to be whoever we are
from our head down to our feet.

The Me Monster can be tamed
long before those teen years set in.
It doesn't mean there won't be shame
or that we will never sin.

But God's promise is that we won't depart
from what we're taught about the way we should
go.
When we're older and get our heads on straight,
we remember and act out what we know.

Just when we need to remember it well,
a little baby with a Me Monster inside may be
born to us.
We'll train it well with Bible stories to tell
and in God's love and grace we will trust.

Thank You, God, for Me Monsters.
They teach us to discipline our souls
so that we can serve others and You
and with the problems of life - just roll!

And thank You for dying on the cross to forgive us
for doing what our Me Monster told us to do;
for helping us to be sorry
so that we instead, start listening to You.

In heaven, there'll be no monsters.
We'll all be one and in one accord -
singing, praising, and serving our Savior
forever with our glorious Lord!

## Say No to Drugs!
### (A Rap Song)

Here comes the pusher with drugs to sell.
If he bothers me, I'm gonna tell.
We'll all get together and yell, yell, yell.

Say - No to Drugs
Say - No to Drugs

Our friends say, " Come on, and have some beer.
We'll have some fun and lots of cheer.
We don't need that stuff, and we'll make it clear."

Say – No to Drugs
Say – No to Drugs

The ads show us cigarettes to smoke.
If we smoke that stuff, I know we'll choke.
We don't need marijuana and we don't need coke.

Say - No to Drugs
Say - No to Drugs

We'll keep our bodies free of drugs and clean.
If we stay healthy, we'll be mean machines.
We'll stay away from junk food, and be real lean.

Say - No to Drugs
Say - No to Drugs

*Well, we hope you liked our little song.*
*If you do what we say - you can't go wrong.*

*Say - No to Drugs*
*Say – No to Drugs ... so long!*

# Woman - God's Feminine Creation

Mother, daughter, sister, and wife;
most every woman fulfills a couple of these roles
during the seasons of her life.

A mother's love is immeasurable;
a loving daughter is faithful and true;
a sister is a forever friend;
and, men, a good wife is God's gift to you.

When I think of a Biblical mother,
I think of Mary, mother of our Lord.
She chose to follow God's path for her
even though it must've been terribly hard.

Thinking of a daughter, Ruth comes to mind.
She was a daughter-in-law faithful and true.
She vowed to follow Naomi, her mother-in-law,
and to stick closer to her than glue.

We all know the Bible story of Baby Moses.
It was his sister, Miriam, who kept him safe and
sound.
He lived to accomplish God's plan to lead his people
out of captivity.
It couldn't have happened without a protective
sister around.

Then there was Sarah, Abraham's faithful wife,
who never deviated from his side in the tiniest.
She surely proved her loyalty
when she bore him a son, Isaac, while in her
nineties.

Of today's mothers, daughters, sisters, and wives,
many are heroes in disguise.
No one works harder for those she loves.
No one shows more care. No one is more wise.

The world should be grateful for good women, you
know,
and learn to help and give credit when due.
A woman's work is never done
and is so beneficial to me and to you.

Thank you, Lord, for women -
for their gentle softness and tender love;
for their special ways with others,
which could come only from You above.

Bless them as they live each day.
Give them love and strength to spare
as they go along life's troubled way;
and show for others so much care.

Amen

# Babies are a Blessing!

## First Born - First Gone

"You've done your best.
Now, I'll do the rest."
That's what the Lord said to me.

"You've done just fine,
but she's really mine.
I just loaned her to you, you see."

"Free choice is a gift I gave to you.
Now I want you to give it to her.
I have a plan for her life -
a beautiful plan
that nothing can deter."

"Just give her love,
and share her joy,
as down life's path she goes."

"For your little girl is a woman now,
and she's blooming like a rose!"

## My Little Girl

I looked at her,
so pink - so new,
as I held her in my arms.
Maybe you've held an infant, too,
and experienced their tiny charms.

And then, it was as if God said to me:
"I'm putting her into your care.
Molding her into what she'll become
is a responsibility we'll share."

She has truly grown in grace and love -
ever obedient and willing to learn.
She has a glow that comes from the Father above,
and for others has love and concern.

Sweetie, I love you will all of my heart,
and I thank you for loving me.
As you grow into a woman, so lovely, so fair,
Praise God for all you will be!

# A Bundle of Joy

Just a bundle of joy
and a bundle of fun,
The baby had arrived
and it all had begun!

She's full of sugar.
She's full of spice.
She's sometimes naughty.
She's sometimes nice.

She drives her sisters right up the wall.
Then she smiles and their hearts melt,
remembering she's small.

She's a gift sent from Heaven.
She's our little girl.
And we wouldn't trade her
for all of the world.

She has a dance in her step
and a song in her heart,
and she truly loves us;
that's the most important part.

Lord, in Your ways let me raise her up -
letting your blessings fill her cup.
Please let her childhood be carefree.
Let her life be a blessing to You and to me.

## Kiki (Mama's Baby)

An answer to prayer;
a gift from God - that's my Kiki girl!
When I'm kissing her whisker area,
I'm in another world.

It's a world of purring and softness;
a world of tenderness and love.
It's the sweetest peaceful blessing
sent from up above.

She curls up right beside me.
She loves the feel of my touch.
We have our sweet dreams side by side.
We love each other so much.

I never before had a pet
that I could call my own;
to show me so much unconditional love
and live beside me in my home.

My daughter found her on the street;
a blue-eyed snowshoe Siamese -
the world not realizing her value -
she's priceless if you please.

I know I don't deserve her.
She's a gift for me - purrrfection.
She's playful and forever a kitten -
so full of tender affection.

114

Her treat is "tuna fish juices."
It has to be Starkist brand in water.
The meows get louder and louder
when it's heated and served slower than it oughta.

My prayer is that she'll be
in the Guinness Book of World Records
for living longer than any other cat -
more days, hours, and seconds!

Thank you, God for Kiki -
for the miracle of her being found on that day,
and for the precious, innocent love
that she has brought my way.

Praise You, Jesus!

# Buddy, a Special Little Dog

He fit into Papa's shirt pocket
the first time that I saw him.
He was the size of a little mouse.
He was an adorable little "Doxie-Pin."

Half miniature Dashshund
and half miniature Pinscher,
he was the cutest little "toy" dog,
and so, so full of adventure.

He stole everyone's heart,
but most especially that of my daughter.
She came to live her life around his needs -
trying to do everything she oughta.

Buddy was the biggest dog I ever knew.
Even though at his heaviest, he weighed 11 pounds.
He'd walk up to a snarling pit bull -
square his legs and stand his ground.

My daughter said she now knew what an angel
looked like
because he was the most precious little dog.
He also looked like a little fawn
when he was sleeping like a log.

He also stole my son-in-law's heart.
They played tug-of-war everyday.
His mom brought Buddy a butter biscuit
from the restaurant where she'd stop along the
way.

He'd scratch at my pocket for a treat.
He knew that's where he'd find one.
He'd look at me and wait for a kiss on his nose.
I called him my "grandpuppy grandson."

He was full of so much vim and vigor.
One day, he jumped off of the couch.
He did that a dozen times a day,
but that time it caused an ouch.

It was more than an ouch, it was an injury.
It caused him pain the rest of his life.
Everyone rallied around him to help him.
With all the help, he still had a good life.

A traveling vet came to the house to attend him.
My daughter slept with him at night.
Her husband built ramps to the sofa top
making sure everything for him was done right.

He was a joy, a blessing sent from above.
We all miss him now that he's gone away,
but we still smile when we remember his style,
and we believe he'll be with us in heaven one day.

*Thank you, God, for Buddy.*
*He brightened up our lives.*
*He was one-of-a-kind - the best kind,*
*and in our hearts, his memory thrives.*

## A Baby Changes Our World

A baby changes our world.
Oh my - how true that is.
My grandson's baby just changed his life
forever and for as long as he lives.

She has him wrapped around her little finger.
She's such a bundle of pink cooing charms.
So new... so sweet... so innocent -
her daddy wants to keep her from all harms.

He's already learning to be a dad.
His son has lassoed his heart,
and he does a great job of taking care of him -
That's the beautiful part.

My grandson and his wife are such great parents.
They complement each other as "Mom and Dad."
That'll mean everything to the children when
grown
as they remember what wonderful childhoods they
had.

Each one in the family - both sides
is just simply thrilled to no end;
to be grandparents, aunts, uncles... what have
ya...
to see new life begin.
Thank , You, God for our baby girl.
What a beautiful gift you gave -

*so perfectly beautiful and healthy;*
*we can't help but rave.*

*But, we thank You for the Baby Jesus, too,*
*a baby who changed our world when He died upon*
*the cross*
*so that we all can go to heaven some day*
*if we believe and receive His forgiveness - no one*
*needs to be lost.*

## "Sweet Sixteen"

Today, our daughter is sweet sixteen,
and a sweet sixteen she is.
The thought that she's almost a woman now
brings my eyes to tears.

There's nothing like the freshness
and sweetness of her face.
She brings to mind a little fawn
as she moves about with such grace.

I saw surprise in her shining eyes
when I presented sixteen red roses.
She thought it had been too much to spend.
She never expects or supposes.

They say that beauty is only skin deep,
but it goes much deeper than that with her.
She has a beauty of soul more precious than gold
and a tender heart, as it were.

She's never brought me trouble...
only joy, love, and happiness.
She's always been a Mama's girl,
showing she loved me best.

She's a kind and gentle sister
to her older and younger sisters alike.
Like the calm in the eye of the storm,
she calms the storms of our life.

*So sweetheart, blow out the candles*
*on your special birthday cake.*
*I hope all your wishes come true,*
*and that the Father above, in His wisdom and love*
*brings good things in the future to you!*

# A Special Girl

My daughter is a special girl -
as special as can be,
and she is as pretty as a peach
with a glow that all can see.

She's fun to be around.
Her laughter fills the air.
She's as funny as a clown.
She makes others forget their cares.

She has a voice that pleases the ears
with a commitment to sing of God in her heart.
The gift of song God gives to her
she gives back to Him - trying to do her part.

She's always been obedient and as I asked,
God has kept her childhood carefree.
Her life has been a blessing to Him,
to others and to me.

She's on the brink of becoming a woman now -
a time of excitement, but also stress.
Please help her moment by moment
to be her very best.

Someday she'll choose a young man, Lord,
to walk with her along life's way.
Guide her, steer her, to make the right choice
so that everything will be okay.

*Help her to get an education*
*so that she'll have a career she'll enjoy -*
*a career that will use the talents*
*and gifts You've given her to employ.*

*Thank You, Lord, for giving us this child*
*to be loved by and to love.*
*Please continue to guide her footsteps*
*and to bless her from above.*

# When I'm With My Little Grandson

When I'm with my little grandson,
I'm as happy as can be!
Maybe that's because I love him,
and he also loves me.

He thanks me when I cook him waffles
or hold him on my lap.
Somehow there just doesn't seem
to be any generation gap.

His big brown eyes and sweet little smile
are irresistible to me.
I know I'll give him anything he asks,
and he knows that too, you see.

No matter how badly I feel
or how unkempt my appearance is,
he's so excited to see me.
At making me feel special, he's a whiz!

His manners are impeccable.
His "sorrys" and thank yous" are surplus,
and sharing candy and TV. with Nannaw
is just simply a must.

Words can't express how I love him.
He's my precious "little man."
Only shared moments can say it
when we walk  hand in hand.

*As he grows into a man, Lord,*
*bless him with laughter, joy, and love*
*and many others blessings*
*sent from You, Lord, up above.*

## Our Niece

A kind heart, intelligence, and beauty,
are all rolled into one.
She has the face of an angel,
and hair that's been kissed by the sun!

She loves helping and building up others;
she's a very special girl.
She always has something good to say
about almost everyone in the world.

She's unselfish, loving and kind,
and always wearing a smile.
She has her own special personality -
her own special kind of style.

Lord, thank You for letting her
be part of our family.
She is a special gift to us -
she's very special to me.

Lord, please bless her with success
as You lead her along life's way,
and show her that true happiness...
is in serving You day by day!

# Our Nephew

He's made of frogs and snails and puppy-dog tails.
He's all boy, it's true.
But you'd better beware - in case you care...
he'll steal your heart from you!

He has a smiling face...
with just the slightest trace
of mischief in his eyes.
He's as honest and true
as his eyes are blue...
as blue as the eastern skies.

The first time I saw him, he was an adorable three.
I fell in love with him, and I think he with me.
He was as loving and sweet as any child can be.
That's my adorable nephew!

Lord, only You know what a boy goes through...
as he works, and laughs, and plays.
He says he was bitten by a gerbil
and nearly by a snake on some recent days!

In life, stand by him, and be his friend.
Guide him with a loving hand...
for we can see, his boyhood will be,
preparation for becoming a man!

# Babies Grow Up

## <u>My Beautiful Granddaughter</u>

My granddaughter is a whiz
at making me feel loved!
I prayed for a beautiful granddaughter,
and God heard my prayers above.

I love it when she comes to visit.
You see, she's a grown woman now.
Many times when the family gathers,
she comes, too, to show her care.

She's certainly a natural beauty -
a brown eyed girl with a long flowing mane of
hair.
She dresses so stylishly and cute
that others can't help but to stare.

She's worked a lot with pre-school kids.
I'm sure she's been a blessing to them all.
To handle all that goes along with that.
I think there would have to be a call.

Thank you for my granddaughter, Lord -
She's brightened up my world.
She's certainly been a blessing to me,
and she's a very special girl.

*Lord, I'd like to ask the best for her.*
*Please send her the desires of her heart.*
*Love, joy, and happiness*
*and all things good that You impart.*

# My Precious Granddaughter

I feel that there's a connection between us -
maybe it's that we both love being a mom.
She makes crafts with the kids and plays with
them.
She loves them a bunch and then some.

She's my granddaughter because she married my
grandson.
I'm so happy to have her in my life.
She's a special part of our family...
always thoughtful towards everyone and also a
very good wife.

I liked her the first time I saw her.
I said a little prayer that she'd be "the one."
She's the mother of my great-granddaughter
and also of my great-grandson.

Give her strength as she goes about her daily
chores -
as she guides the small ones You've entrusted into
her care.
Give her rest, love, and happiness
and enough joy that she can share.

Thank You, Lord, for my granddaughter.
She blesses our family with her love.
Send many showers of blessing upon her
from You, Lord, up above.

# Handsome in Every Way

" I wish I could take her home with me,"
he said as he scooped her up into his arms.
He was my daughter's fiancée
and so full of "princely" charms.

"He's the most handsome man I've ever seen,"
she had said the first time they met.
She still says so, and nobody disagrees.
It's obvious he hasn't lost his good looks yet.

Thirty-three years later, she calls him her, "Honey
Bear."
He scooped her up, married her and took her
away.
He has always given her the very best care
each and every day.

He's worked hard to make a living -
always loving, always giving;
never complaining about his need for rest;
always wanting her to have the best.

He sells boilers to large companies.
His many sales show his persuasion's worth.
He used to get greasy working on them,
from the inside out, he knows his turf.

He's helped her raise their son who has given them grandkids.
He's called "Grampy" by a little boy and girl.
I want you to know, by the love they show,
he's the best Grampy in all of the world.

He's also a wonderful " son" to us
always showing he loves the rest of the family, too.
He's surely passed the test of time
showing a heart that's true blue.

Thank you for this good man, Lord,
who has filled our daughter's life with love.
Keep watching over him with all things good
sent from You, Lord, up above.

# A Special Young Man

What unexpected joy -
He came into our life!
He was to become my son-in-law
because my daughter became his wife.

He honored me by calling me "Mama,"
and I definitely call him my son.
A very loving relationship
had most truly begun.

He was seeking the truth about Jesus -
about how to be born again.
Jesus never lets you down when you seek Him.
He prayed the sinner's prayer and his new life
began!

He has a special love for my daughter.
When we pray family blessing at our house,
He always thanks God for her -
expressing gratitude for a good spouse.

I always wanted a little granddaughter
to love and to give love back to me.
His daughter has accepted that role,
and I treasure her love, you see.

*He is the daddy of four of my grandpuppies.*
*He and my daughter have a passion for dogs.*
*They love and discipline them as children.*
*I couldn't have picked better from catalogs.*

*He is such a hard worker at his job.*
*He takes pride in doing his best.*
*It takes a gifted artist to accomplish what he does,*
*and he puts productivity and excellence to the test.*

*Thank you, God, for our "son" -*
*for bringing him into our lives.*
*Bless him with peace, love, and happiness,*
*and give him all for which he strives.*

# Kind, Loving, and True

I was sitting in the waiting area of the D.M.V.
and couldn't help but hear the young man behind
me.
It was most unusual for a young man his age
to be speaking to an elderly man so very kindly.

He's the kindest person I've ever known -
always doing for others and putting them first.
He and my youngest daughter are married for 12
years now,
having promised for better or worse.

Being married to him is never worse - only better
for her.
He's a wonderful husband and man.
He keeps busy making life exciting and fun -
keeping nice surprises coming as much as he can!

He shows integrity in all that he does.
No one works harder to take care of family.
He thinks ahead and keeps up with duties -
sidetracking any future calamity.

He's an engineer and quite an artist.
His designs are great to see.
Beauty and functionality rolled into one -
he's decidedly the best he can be.

He's loving, kind, and generous -
always helping everyone out.
He's crazy about their two little dogs,
and that they are crazy about him too - is no
doubt.

It's wonderful to see our daughter so happy.
She says, "He's the best husband in the world, "
and it's wonderful to have him for a "son" -
married to our little girl.

Bless him Lord; You see his heart.
You know he is loving, kind and true.
Lift him up - keep him well and strong
because when he serves others, he's serving You.

# My Husband

Like a Knight in shining armor,
he swept into my life.
He helped me with my problems.
He helped me with my strife.

And then, he said, "I love you.
All my life I've looked for you."
Oh Lord, it's happening all so quickly.
Can this love be true?

Then came an answer to my prayer
as my heart was filled with love.
"This is the man I've sent to you.
I've heard your prayers above."

We prayerfully decided on marriage,
but many obstacles were in the way.
We battled through and clung to love
until our wedding day.

And through the years succeeding,
we've had blessings by the score -
as we have gratefully received
all that God has had in store.

Continue to lead us on, dear Lord
by the Holy Spirit's power.
Keep our marriage safe and secure
through each and every hour.

# Some Friends _Are_ Family

## One True Friend

When I was just a very young girl,
someone said to me,
"If you find just one true friend in this world -
how lucky you will be."

I asked the Lord to send that friend,
and I looked for her along the way.
Many, many, years went by,
but He answered that prayer one day.

It's wonderful to have a friend like mine,
who even overlooks my faults.
We've shared in joy - we've shared in pain.
The love she gives me can't be bought.

Thank you, Lord, for my friend so true,
and for everything we share.
We know we're really sisters in You,
because of the way we care!

Lead her on, Dear Jesus,
to put You first, in love,
and shower her with blessings
from You, Lord, up above!

## A Special Couple

There is a special couple
my husband speaks of much.
They reached out to him as a boy
with such a loving touch.

They helped to teach him right from wrong...
for his own dad had passed away,
and they also helped to guide him on...
to become the man he is today.

They had children of their own,
but they were still willing to share.
They shared the blessing of a farm and home,
because they knew how to care.

The Mr. was always patient with him...
no matter what troubles he caused.
He says if it hadn't been for his kind discipline,
he might have ended up behind bars.

The Mrs. let him watch TV
and play with her little girls.
He has as much respect for her way of living,
as for anyone's in the world.

Thank You, Lord, for this special pair,
and the good examples they were to him.
It was such a blessing that they were there...
for he's patterned his life after them.

*Lord, pour out your blessings on this couple.*
*Overflow their lives with joy,*
*and never, ever, let them forget...*
*what they added to the life of a boy!*

## We love Dr. B.

"My little girl is very sick,"
I told the girl next door.
 I need to find a doctor quick.
It's a problem I can't ignore."

She said, "I know one who'll take care of her.
He is the very best there is.
His name is Dr. B.,
and he's just great with kids."

We found he is the kind of doctor
who goes the extra mile.
He has a natural gift for doctoring,
and an ever-present smile.

Through the years, as a mother,
I've learned to trust in his care,
and he has never let me down…
Thank God, he's always there.

Yes, thank you, Lord, for Dr. B.
and the care he's given my girls.
He's been a doctor and a friend,
and he's brightened up our world.

We'd like to ask the best for him -
in his practice and his life.
Give him joy, good health, and love,
and keep him free from strife.

# L.J. Johns - God's Genteel Pastor

Yesterday, he left this world
where there's sickness and there's pain -
to enter into heaven's glory
where our loss is his gain.

Oh, can you even try to imagine
what L.J. is experiencing now...
in the arms of his Savior
and with loved ones already there?

We didn't want to see him leave;
the pain was just too great.
But we can know when we get there,
he'll be waiting for us at the gate!

Oh, gates of pearl and streets of gold
as promised in God's Word,
if we'll repent of our sin and believe in Jesus
in case you haven't heard.

Pastor L.J. Johns would want you to know
that's what his whole life was about.
He preached the saving Word of God,
so we all might hear the Victor's shout.

He showed such refinement in his manner -
his speech so eloquent and polite.
He blended this with a country boy's heart -
raised by "a sweet little widow lady" just right.

*He was brought up so deep in the country*
*that he said they had to pipe the light in.*
*And he was just a teen*
*when God's call for him to preach began.*

*Oh, what a loving husband he was!*
*Jeanne was always his beloved bride -*
*over sixty years of family and ministry together,*
*gently riding life's turbulent tide.*

*Four daughters and a son God bestowed on them.*
*L.J. was such a sensitive dad.*
*He was a loving grandfather to his own, my*
*daughter, and others*
*making the children of his church so glad.*

*Thank You, God, for giving us L.J.*
*to love and be loved by him.*
*We're all so happy that in life, he passed our way,*
*with so much of Your love in his heart to spend.*

# About the Author

Janie Carter was born prematurely on the 6th anniversary of the day her father had a life-threatening accident and was told he could never produce another child. Her heart stopped beating on the operating table at age 3, but she revived and enjoyed a wonderful childhood! At age 18, she repented of her sins and accepted the Lord as her Savior. That was the day she fell in love with Jesus!

From that day forward, she has embraced the Christian life with passion - promising God to share the good news of Jesus' gift of eternal salvation, and knowledge of the Holy Spirit whom He sent to comfort, guide, and empower us! Teaching and testimonies of God's goodness have characterized her life. The Lord has turned all of her scars into stars, and she loves sharing how He can do the same in others' lives as well!

35 years ago, the Holy Spirit started "whispering poems" to her to inspire and minister to others. This book is a collection of 73 of those poems.

She is so thankful for her loving, supportive husband, three wonderful daughters and sons-in-law, two terrific grandchildren and granddaughter- in-law, and two absolutely amazing great-grandchildren! She and her husband live in Richmond, Virginia.

*For you have been born again, not of perishable seed, but of imperishable,*
*though the living and enduring Word of God.*
*1 Peter 1: 23 (NIV)*

If you enjoyed this book, would you please take just a minute or two to leave a positive review? Your valuable feedback helps others make a quality decision about purchasing or sharing these poems. Thank you kindly and God bless you!

65588260R00092

Made in the USA
Middletown, DE
04 September 2019